Favorite
HERBS

KÖNEMANN

–*BASIL*–

Sweet basil, with its delicious flavor and scent, is a versatile herb. It is especially renowned for its affinity with tomatoes. It is also excellent with eggplant, zucchini, squash, and spinach. The chopped leaves, added towards the end of the cooking time, give a wonderful flavor to many soups.

Basil is also a favorite flavor in chicken and pasta dishes and can be tossed with lettuce in green salads.

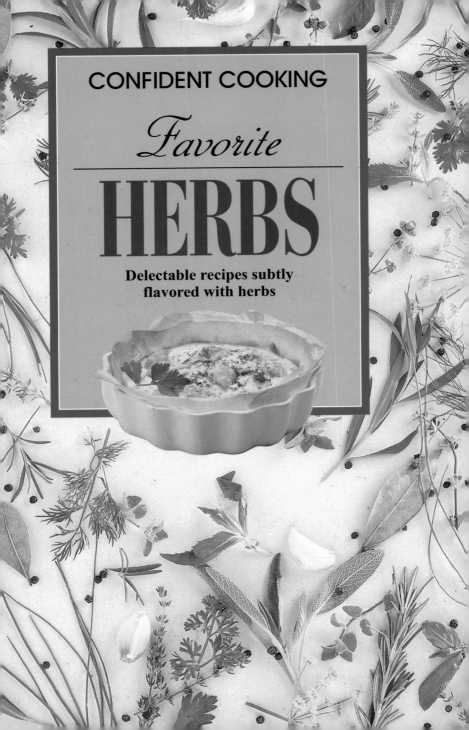

CONFIDENT COOKING

Favorite

HERBS

**Delectable recipes subtly
flavored with herbs**

USEFUL INFORMATION

Easy

A little care needed

More care needed

All our recipes are thoroughly tested. Standard metric measuring cups and spoons are used in the development of our recipes. All cup and spoon measurements are level. We have used 60 g eggs in all recipes. Sizes of cans vary from manufacturer to manufacturer and between countries; use the can size closest to the one suggested in the recipes.

Weights and Measures				
3 teaspoons	=	1 tablespoon	1 tablespoon	= ½ fluid ounce
4 tablespoons	=	¼ cup	1 cup	= 8 fluid ounces
5 ½ tablespoons	=	⅓ cup	1 cup	= ½ US-pint
8 tablespoons	=	½ cup	2 cups	= 1 US-pint
11 tablespoons	=	⅔ cup	4 cups	= 1 quart
12 tablespoons	=	¾ cup	2 US-pints	= 1 quart
16 tablespoons	=	1 cup	4 quarts	= 3 ¾ liters
1 tablespoon	=	20 milliliters	¼ pound	= 125 grams
1 cup	=	250 milliliters	½ pound	= 250 grams
1.06 quart	=	1 liter	¾ pound	= 375 grams
			1 pound	= 500 grams

This US-edition first published 1998 by
KÖNEMANN Verlagsgesellschaft mbH
Bonner Str. 126, D-50968 Cologne
Printing and binding: Sing Cheong Printing Co., Ltd.
Printed in Hong Kong, China
ISBN 3-8290-0373-0

Ricotta and Basil Lasagna

Preparation time:
 15 minutes
Cooking time:
 35 to 40 minutes
Serves 6 to 8

8 lasagna noodles
2 cloves garlic, crushed
1/4 cup butter or
 margarine
3 tablespoons all-
 purpose flour
Pinch nutmeg
2 cups milk
2 tablespoons finely
 chopped fresh basil
2 cups ricotta cheese
1 cup grated Parmesan
 cheese
Salt and white pepper
8-ounce package sliced
 mozzarella cheese
2 tablespoons chopped
 fresh basil

1 Cook noodles according to package directions; drain. In a saucepan cook garlic in butter or margarine till tender. Stir in flour and nutmeg. Add milk. Cook and stir till thickened and bubbly. Cook and stir for 1 minute more.
2 Remove sauce from heat. Stir in 2 tablespoons finely chopped basil. Add ricotta cheese and half of the Parmesan cheese, stirring till well combined. Season to taste with salt and pepper.
3 Layer half the cooked noodles in a 12 x 7 1/2 x 2-inch baking dish. Spread with half of the ricotta mixture and top with half of the mozzarella cheese. Sprinkle with 1 tablespoon of the chopped basil. Repeat layers. Sprinkle the remaining Parmesan cheese on top.
4 Bake in a 375° oven for 30 to 35 minutes or till heated through. Let stand 10 minutes.

PESTO

Pesto is another method of preserving aromatic fresh basil. This is a sauce from the Mediterranean. Basil leaves are pounded together with pine nuts, garlic, olive oil, and fresh Parmesan cheese. Originally pesto was made by using a mortar and pestle. Today, it is commonly blended in a food processor. The basil mixture can be placed in an airtight container and refrigerated for a few days or stored in the freezer for several months.

Ricotta and Basil Lasagna

Country Fresh Vegetable Soup

Preparation time:
  15 minutes
Cooking time:
  20 minutes
Serves 4

2 tablespoons butter or
  margarine
2 ounces Canadian-
  style bacon, chopped
1 small onion, chopped
1 leek, cleaned and
  sliced
1 clove garlic, crushed
1 sprig fresh rosemary,
  coarsely chopped
2 tomatoes, coarsely
  chopped
1 bunch fresh
  asparagus, trimmed
  and chopped
5 ounces fresh green
  beans, trimmed and
  chopped
2 potatoes, peeled and
  chopped
2 zucchini, chopped
2 stalks celery, chopped
6 cups chicken or
  vegetable broth
1 cup long grain rice
1 small bunch fresh
  basil, finely chopped
1/2 cup grated Parmesan
  cheese
Grated Parmesan
  cheese (optional)

1 In a large saucepan
melt butter or
margarine. Add bacon,
onion, leek, garlic, and
rosemary. Cook and stir
till onion is tender.

2 Stir in tomatoes, asparagus, green beans, potatoes, zucchini, and celery. Add broth. Bring to a boil; add rice. Return to a boil; reduce heat. Cover and simmer for 20 minutes or till rice is tender.

3 Remove from heat and stir in basil and 1/2 cup Parmesan cheese. Let stand 5 minutes. Serve with additional Parmesan cheese, if desired.

Variations
The variations on this classic soup are endless, depending on the vegetables available and the cook's imagination. In fact, any vegetables in season could end up in this soup pot.

Macaroni can replace the rice and dried herbs can replace the fresh. If using dried herbs, use 1/2 teaspoon dried rosemary and 1 tablespoon dried basil, crushed.

Pesto

Preparation time:
  10 minutes
Cooking time:
  None
Makes about 2/3 cup

1 *cup firmly packed fresh basil leaves*

2 *cloves garlic*
1/2 *cup grated*
  Parmesan cheese
2 *tablespoons pine*
  nuts, lightly toasted
1 *teaspoon toasted*
  bread crumbs
1/3 *cup olive oil*

1 In a food processor or blender combine basil, garlic, Parmesan cheese, pine nuts, and bread crumbs. Cover and process or blend till a paste forms. Stop machine and scrape down sides when necessary.

2 With machine running, gradually add oil and process or blend till well combined. Cover and store in the refrigerator or freezer. Toss pesto with hot cooked pasta or spaghetti squash.

STORING PESTO
Pesto can be kept 5 to 7 days in refrigerator if the surface is covered with a thin layer of olive oil. Or, it can be frozen for several months, but omit the cheese and stir it into the pesto once it thaws. Enthusiasts maintain that pesto should be made just before using because storing the sauce decreases its quality.

Country Fresh Vegetable Soup

–*BAY*–

Bay leaves are a traditional ingredient in bouquet garni. Bay leaves, on their own, flavor soups and casseroles, fish and seafood, meat and poultry, marinades, and terrines. An old-fashioned way to flavor pudding was to arrange a fresh bay leaf on top before placing it in the oven. The subtle and unusual flavor of the bay leaf would give piquancy to the sweet dish. Any time you cook with bay leaves, be sure to discard them before serving.

BOUQUET GARNI

Bay leaves are one of the important ingredients in making a bouquet garni. The other herbs used are parsley, marjoram, and thyme. Peppercorns may also be added, if desired. When used fresh, these herbs are tied together and put in casseroles, soups, and stews. When dried herbs are used, they are crumbled to make a blend, tied in a piece of cheesecloth, and added to the food at the beginning of the cooking. Discard the fresh or dried bouquet garni before serving the meal.

Duck and Chicken Liver Pâté

desired. Gather up corners and tie with a piece of string. Make sure the string is long enough to drop into a large saucepan, leaving enough string to hang over the edge to pull out.

Note: A collection of homemade bouquet garni, packed neatly in a box or decorative container, makes a thoughtful gift for someone who likes to cook.

Duck and Chicken Liver Pâté

Preparation time:
  8 minutes
Cooking time:
  5 minutes
Chilling time:
  1 to 2 hours
Serves 6

8 ounces duck or
  chicken livers
8 ounces chicken livers
1 cup unsalted butter
1 large onion, chopped
2 cloves garlic,
  crushed
1/4 cup chopped mixed
  fresh herbs: sage,
  parsley, marjoram,
  parsley, and chives
3 tablespoons Grand
  Marnier
Clarified butter (see
  next page)
Bay leaves

Peppercorns
Crusty bread slices or
  melba toast

1 Remove fat or dark spots from livers. In a heavy large skillet melt butter. Cook onion in butter till tender. Add garlic. Cook for 1 minute; remove onion and garlic with slotted spoon to a food processor.
2 In same pan cook livers, a few at a time, about 3 minutes or till no longer pink. Transfer to food processor with onion and garlic.
3 Cover and blend till smooth. Add herbs and Grand Marnier. Cover and blend till smooth.
4 Pour mixture into a terrine or serving dish. Let stand 5 minutes. Arrange bay leaves and peppercorns over surface of pâté. Carefully spoon clarified butter over pâté. Chill for 1 to 2 hours or till set. Serve with slices of bread or melba toast (see next page).

Variations
You can use 1 pound chicken livers instead of a combination of chicken and duck livers. Port or brandy can be used to replace the Grand Marnier.

Bouquet Garni

1 bay leaf
2 sprigs fresh parsley
1 sprig fresh thyme
1 sprig fresh marjoram
Peppercorns (optional)

1 Chop herbs and place in the middle of a piece of cheesecloth. Add peppercorns, if

–*CHIVES*–

MELBA TOAST

Here's how to make your own melba toast to serve with pâté. Remove crusts from sliced white bread. Flatten each slice with a rolling pin. Cut each slice diagonally into quarters, making 4 triangles. Place in a single layer on a baking sheet. Bake in a 400° oven for 10 to 15 minutes or till golden brown.

CLARIFIED BUTTER

To clarify butter, melt over low heat in a saucepan. Slowly pour over pâté, leaving milky residue in saucepan. This seals the pâté, allowing you to store it in the refrigerator for up to 5 days.

DRYING YOUR OWN

If you have access to fresh bay leaves (dry ones are available in your supermarket herb section) you can use them fresh throughout the year or dry them. To dry, pick leaves from stalks and spread them out onto a wire rack. Let stand at room temperature till dry. Or, bunch the leaves together and hang them in an airy place to dry.

Finely chopped chives go into all kinds of salads, egg dishes, cream cheese, sauces, and mayonnaise. They also make an attractive garnish, especially the chive blossoms.

Fines Herbes, the traditional French flavoring in omelettes, is equal parts onion chives, parsley, tarragon, and chervil – all finely chopped.

Creamy Salmon Mousse

Preparation time:
  20 minutes
Chilling time:
  Several hours or
  overnight
Cooking time:
  None
Serves 6

2 x 6³/4-ounce cans
  boneless skinless
  salmon, drained and
  flaked
¹/2 cup plain yogurt
¹/2 cup cottage
  cheese
2 tablespoons lemon
  juice
1 tablespoon white
  vinegar
1 tablespoon chopped
  fresh chives
1 envelope unflavored
  gelatin
1 cup hot water
1 cup whipping cream

1 In a food processor
or blender combine
salmon, yogurt, cottage
cheese, lemon juice,
and vinegar. Cover and
process or blend till
smooth. Transfer to a
large bowl; stir in
chives.
2 Sprinkle gelatin over
hot water. Stir till
dissolved. Stir a few
tablespoons salmon
mixture into gelatin

*Creamy Salmon
Mousse*

mixture. Add all of gelatin mixture to salmon mixture. Whisk till well combined. Cool for 10 to 15 minutes.

3 In a bowl beat whipping cream with an electric mixer till soft peaks form. Fold into salmon mixture. Pour into a lightly oiled 3-cup mold. Cover and chill several hours or overnight till set.

4 To serve, loosen edges with a knife. Dip mold in a bowl of warm water; shake mold slightly to loosen. Place a chilled serving plate over mold; invert onto plate. Serve with melba toast, vegetables, and fresh herbs.

Variation
Other fresh herbs, chopped gherkins, or capers can be added to this savory mousse.

Watchpoints
To dissolve gelatin easily, stir it into the hot water with a wire whisk.

The gelatin and salmon mixture should be at the same temperature to make it easier to combine them.

To successfully unmold your mousse, place the mold in the freezer for a few minutes before pouring in the salmon mixture. This, along with lightly oiling the mold, prevents sticking.

Chicken Chive Surprise

Preparation time:
  15 minutes
Freezing time:
  1 hour
Chilling time:
  1 to 2 hours
Cooking time:
  8 to 10 minutes
Serves 4

1 pound boneless, skinless chicken breasts
3/4 cup butter or margarine, softened
1 egg yolk
3 tablespoons finely chopped fresh chives
1 clove garlic, crushed
1/2 cup all-purpose flour
2 eggs, beaten
Fine dry bread crumbs
Oil for deep-fat frying

1 Rinse chicken and pat dry with paper towels. If necessary, cut chicken into four portions. Place on cutting board and pound with the flat side of a meat mallet to about 1/4-inch thickness. Set aside.

2 In a bowl stir together butter or margarine, egg yolk, chives, and garlic. Form into a long cylinder. Wrap in plastic wrap and freeze about 1 hour or till very hard. Cut into 4 equal portions.

3 Wrap one chicken breast around one butter portion, securing with toothpicks. Toss in flour and shake off any excess. Dip in eggs and coat with bread crumbs. Refrigerate for 1 to 2 hours.

Chicken Chive Surprise

Cook's Tips
Steps 1 and 2 of this recipe can be prepared ahead of time.

You can double the amount of herb butter and freeze half to use later as a delicious topping for fish or steaks (omit egg yolk).

STORING CHIVES
Fresh chives may be frozen for several months or made into herb butter and stored in the refrigerator or freezer.

RETAINING FLAVOUR
The flavor of chives is destroyed if they are cooked too long. For best flavor, add them during the last 5 or 10 minutes of cooking.

4 Fry chicken breasts in hot oil (375°) for 5 to 8 minutes or till golden brown and chicken is no longer pink.

Watchpoint
Do not reheat this dish or try to keep it warm for a long time because the butter will melt out of the chicken. If the oil for cooking gets too hot, add a little more oil to cool it down.

11

–*CORIANDER*–

The lacy, feathery foliage of coriander has a unique scent that is penetrating and lively. It is also know as cilantro or Chinese parsley and belongs to the same family as parsley, caraway, dill, and fennel.

Add the chopped leaves sparingly to poultry, lamb, and vegetable dishes. Coriander also teams well with Asian-style dishes, Southwest dishes, pears, and mangoes. The seeds are often used to flavor oils and vinegars.

Skewered Coriander Seafood Salad

Preparation time:
  10 minutes
Marinating time:
  30 minutes
Cooking time:
  10 minutes
Serves 6

2 *pounds firm white fish fillets*
1 *cup plain yogurt*
3 *tablespoons lemon juice*
3 *cloves garlic, crushed*

2 *tablespoons all-purpose flour*
1 *tablespoon finely grated gingerroot*
1 *teaspoon garam marsala (available at Asian markets)*
1 *teaspoon chopped fresh coriander or cilantro*
1/2 *teaspoon chili powder*

Salad
2 *carrots*
2 *cucumbers*
10 *snow peas*
1 *red bell pepper, seeded*

1 Rinse fish and pat dry; cut into 1-inch cubes. In a shallow glass dish stir together yogurt, lemon juice, garlic, flour, gingerroot, garam marsala, coriander or cilantro, and chili powder. Add fish, tossing to coat. Cover; marinate in the refrigerator for 30 minutes.
2 Preheat broiler. Thread fish on skewers, using about 4 or 5 cubes per skewer. Place on the unheated rack of a broiler pan. Broil 4 to 6 inches from the heat about 10 minutes or till fish flakes easily with a fork, turning skewers occasionally.
3 While fish cooks, for the salad cut carrots, cucumbers, snow peas, and bell pepper into julienne strips. Toss

Skewered Coriander Seafood Salad

together. To serve, let skewers cool slightly. Arrange skewers on top of vegetables.

Variations
You can use a variety of seafood in this salad in combination with, or instead of, the fish. Try prawns or shrimp, crab, or crawfish for a party or other special occasion meal.

Baked Halibut with a Citrus and Coriander Sauce

Preparation time:
  5 minutes
Cooking time:
  15 to 20 minutes
Serves 4

8 ounces penne pasta
3 tablespoons cooking oil

4 *small halibut steaks*
2 *cloves garlic,*
  crushed
2/3 *cup tomato*
  purée
3 *tablespoons lime,*
  lemon, or orange
  juice or combination
1 *tablespoon chopped*
  fresh coriander or
  cilantro
Red pepper flakes
Fresh coriander or
  cilantro sprigs

13

1 Cook penne according to package directions till al dente. Drain, transfer to an ovenproof dish, and stir in 1 tablespoon of the oil.

2 In a skillet heat the remaining 2 tablespoons oil over medium-high heat. Add halibut to hot skillet. Brown fish on both sides. Transfer to ovenproof dish over cooked pasta.

3 In same skillet cook garlic till tender (add more oil, if necessary). Stir in tomato purée, juice, coriander or cilantro, and red pepper flakes. Bring to a boil; remove from heat. Pour over fish and pasta, covering pasta completely.

4 Cover and bake in 400° oven for 15 to 20 minutes or till fish flakes easily when tested with a fork. Garnish with sprigs of fresh coriander or cilantro.

Variations
Fresh dill or basil can be used instead of coriander. Rice can replace the pasta.

Watchpoint
Fish is done when the flesh is white and opaque and it flakes easily when tested with a fork.

CORIANDER SEEDS
Coriander seeds have many uses in cooking. The aromatic seeds are mixed with other whole spices in pickling blends. Ground seeds flavor fish, poultry, and meat dishes. They are also used in fruit cakes, gingerbread, biscuits, pastry, and bread. Coriander seeds taste excellent sprinkled over baked apples, pears, and peaches. Or, try sprinkling a pinch of coriander over hot cooked vegetables.

The clean, spicy scent of dill is pleasing to most people. Dill may be used to replace parsley, mint, basil, or tarragon. Dill is delicious combined with roasted meat and can be sprinkled liberally on

Dill-Mustard Potato Salad

Preparation time:
  10 minutes
Cooking time:
  15 minutes
Chilling time:
  Several hours
Serves 6

8 cups chicken broth
2 pounds new white or
  red potatoes
1/2 cup vegetable oil
1/4 cup Dijon mustard
2 tablespoons chopped
  fresh dill or 2 teaspoons
  dried dillweed
1 teaspoon red wine
  vinegar

1 teaspoon lemon juice
1/2 cup sour cream
Freshly ground pepper
3 stalks celery, sliced
1 onion, thinly sliced
  and separated into
  rings
1/2 bunch fresh chives,
  snipped

1 In a large saucepan
combine chicken broth
and potatoes. Bring to
a boil; reduce heat.
Cover and simmer
about 15 minutes or
till potatoes are tender.
Drain immediately and
rinse with cold water.
Drain potatoes well
and set aside.
2 For dressing, in a
food processor or

Dill-Mustard Potato Salad

lamb, veal, and chicken.
Add dill to gravy,
sprinkle it over steamed
vegetables, add it to
seafood casseroles, or
make a tasty soup with
it. Don't forget to use
chopped fresh dill in
omelettes and salads.

blender combine 3 tablespoons of the oil, mustard, dill, vinegar, and lemon juice. Cover and process or blend till well combined. With machine running, slowly add remaining oil till well combined. Add sour cream and process or blend till combined. Season with pepper.

3   Quarter potatoes and place in a salad bowl with celery and onion. Pour dressing over potato mixture, tossing gently to coat. Cover and chill for several hours. Garnish with chives.

Variations
This recipe is delicious served hot or cold. Capers can be used to replace the dill and you can add chopped cooked bacon or sliced hard-cooked eggs to make an interesting change to the recipe.

Serving suggestions
Serve Dill-Mustard Potato Salad as an accompaniment to meat, poultry, or fish.

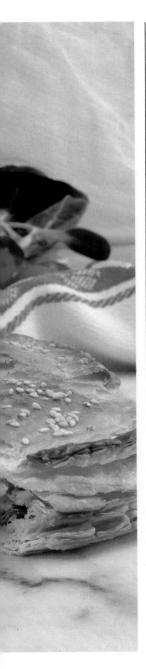

Salmon Pie

Preparation time:
  15 minutes
Cooking time:
  15 to 20 minutes
Serves 4

17¼-*ounce package
(2 sheets) frozen puff
pastry, thawed*
2 x 6¾-*ounce cans
boneless skinless
salmon, drained and
flaked*
1 *cup cooked long
grain rice*
6 *shallots, diagonally
sliced*
3 *tablespoons tiny
sprigs fresh dill*
*Finely shredded peel of
lime or lemon*
*Salt and freshly ground
pepper*
1 *egg, beaten*
Sesame seed

1 Place pastry sheets
on a lightly floured
surface. Cut a 9½-inch
circle from each sheet,
using a dinner plate or
saucepan lid as a guide.
Place one circle on a
greased baking sheet.
2 For filling, in a bowl
stir together salmon,
rice, shallots, dill, and
peel. Season with salt
and pepper. Spread
filling over pastry circle,
leaving 1-inch border.
3 Moisten edge of
bottom pastry with

water. Place second
pastry circle on top.
Firmly press edges to
seal. With the blunt end
of a knife, press and lift
pastry at intervals to
decorate rim and help
provide "lift" during
baking. Brush top of
pastry with egg and
sprinkle with sesame
seed. Gently pierce top
of pastry with a fork to
allow steam to escape.
4 Bake in a 450° oven
for 15 to 20 minutes or
till pastry is crisp and
golden brown and
filling is heated
through. Cool slightly
before cutting into
wedges.

Variations
Tuna can replace
salmon. You can add a
chopped hard-cooked
egg to the filling.

Watchpoint
Do not thaw and
refreeze puff pastry.
This will decrease the
quality of the pastry
and cause it to crack
when used later.

A GOOD COMPANION
Planting dill in your
vegetable garden is
said to help corn,
lettuce, cucumbers,
and cabbages grow.
The dill blossoms
often attract honey
bees.

Salmon Pie

–*Fennel*–

Traditionally served with fish, fennel is delicious with many other dishes. Chop fennel finely and sprinkle over salads or steamed vegetables. Stir it into spaghetti sauce or cooked rice. Fennel seeds, like dill and caraway, are said to be good for digestion. Fennel seeds may be used whole or ground and have a strong anise flavor.

Grilled Fish with Fennel

Preparation time:
  10 minutes
Marinating time:
  1 hour
Cooking time:
  15 to 20 minutes
Serves 4

Fresh fennel stalks
4 medium drawn rainbow
  trout or coho salmon

1/2 cup olive oil
Juice of 1 lemon
1/4 cup Cognac or
  brandy
2 cloves garlic, crushed
Salt and freshly ground
  pepper
1 leek, cleaned and
  sliced

1 Place 1 fennel stalk inside each fish. With a sharp knife score fish with three 2-inch slashes on each side.
2 In a bowl stir together

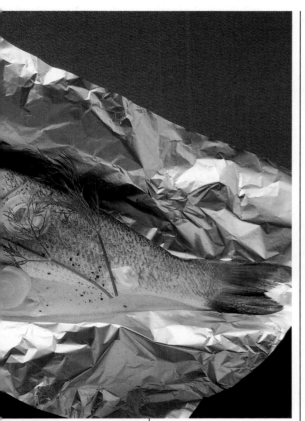

Grilled Fish with Fennel

easily with a fork.
Note: Drawn fish is a whole fish minus its internal organs. It may need to be scaled.

Variations
You can broil the fish for this recipe instead of grilling. Place dried fennel on the rack of an unheated broiler pan. Place fish on rack. Broil fish about 4 inches from the heat 5 to 7 minutes on each side or till fish flakes easily when tested with a fork.

Watchpoints
If necessary, when buying your fish, ask the fishmonger or butcher to scale and clean it for you. To ensure the fish is fresh, the eyes should be clear, tail and fins intact, and flesh moist.

oil, lemon juice, Cognac or brandy, and garlic. Pour over fish. Season with salt and pepper. Cover and marinate in the refrigerator for 1 hour.
3 If desired, place remaining fennel stalks on a baking sheet and dry in a 200° oven. Drain fish. Tear off 4 pieces of heavy-duty foil large enough to hold each fish. Prick a few holes in the foil.

Arrange fish on foil, bringing sides up around fish, but not sealing fish. Add sliced leek.
4 In a covered grill arrange preheated coals around a foil drip pan. Test for hot heat above pan. If desired, place the dried fennel stalks on the preheated coals. Place fish on rack over center of drip pan, but not over coals. Lower grill hood. Grill for 15 to 20 minutes or till fish flakes

ITALIAN DELICACY
The swollen base of fennel is quite a delicacy and is served in Italian restaurants when it is in season. It is cut into circles or vertical slices and tossed in oil and vinegar and seasoned with freshly ground pepper.

–GARLIC–

Garlic is a pungent bulb related to the onion. It imparts its own unique and savory aroma to many types of cooking. Garlic is a common ingredient in meat dishes, poultry dishes, fish and seafood dishes, stews, egg dishes, vegetable dishes, salads, breads, sauces, mayonnaise, and salad dressings.

Beef Casserole with Mushrooms and Wine

Preparation time:
  15 minutes
Cooking time:
  2 hours
Serves 6

Olive oil
2 pounds boneless top
  round steak, trimmed
  of fat and cut into
  2-inch cubes

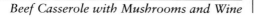

Beef Casserole with Mushrooms and Wine

1 onion, sliced
1 tablespoon all-
purpose flour
3 tablespoons brandy,
warmed
2 cloves garlic, crushed
Bouquet garni
Freshly ground pepper
2 cups homemade beef
stock or canned beef
broth
1 cup dry red wine
20 small white onions
or frozen pearl onions
6 ounces mushrooms,
thickly sliced
Chopped fresh parsley

1 In a large skillet heat about 2 tablespoon olive oil. Cook meat in batches over medium-high heat till brown. Remove. Add onions to skillet, adding more oil, if necessary. Cook; stir till tender. Stir in flour. Add brandy and ignite. When flames subside, reduce heat.

2 Add garlic and bouquet garni to skillet. Season generously with pepper. Return meat to skillet; add beef stock and wine. Bring to a boil; remove from heat.

3 Transfer meat mixture to large casserole. Cover; bake in a 325° oven for 1½ hours or till tender, stirring occasionally. Add onions and mushrooms; bake, covered, for 30 minutes.

4 Before serving, discard bouquet garni. Sprinkle with parsley; serve from casserole.

Nutrition Note
Any health-conscious cook will enjoy this recipe since the bouquet garni adds flavor without salt, monosaturated olive oil is used instead of high cholesterol butter, and the fat is trimmed from the meat before cooking. To make the casserole gluten-free, omit the flour and use 1/2 teaspoon cornstarch.

Serving suggestion
Serve this hearty casserole with cooked brown rice, a tossed green salad, and a loaf of crusty whole grain bread. You can make it in advance and refrigerate it for 2 or 3 days or freeze it for several weeks.

USES FOR GARLIC
A clove of raw garlic rubbed around the inside of a wooden salad bowl gives a subtle garlic flavor to the salad tossed in the bowl. Garlic marries well with lamb, pork, veal, beef, tomatoes, eggplant, Asian dishes, and curries. When making garlic bread, mash a few savory herbs into the butter with the garlic to make herb garlic bread.

Pork Tenderloin with Honey Ginger Glaze

Preparation time:
 8 minutes
Cooking time:
 25 to 30 minutes
Serves 4

1 pound pork tenderloin
1 tablespoon cooking oil
1/3 cup honey
2 cloves garlic, crushed
2 tablespoons light soy sauce
2 teaspoons grated gingerroot
2 tablespoons sesame seed, toasted

1 Trim pork of all visible fat. In a skillet heat oil over medium-high heat. Brown pork on all sides in hot skillet. Transfer to a baking dish. Bake, uncovered, in a 350° oven for 25 to 30 minutes or till a meat thermometer registers 160°.
2 Meanwhile, clean skillet. In same skillet combine honey, garlic, soy sauce, and gingerroot. Cook over low heat till heated through. Slice pork diagonally and toss in honey mixture. Sprinkle with sesame seed.

Spanish-Style Fish

Preparation time:
 10 minutes
Cooking time:
 20 minutes
Serves 4

11/2 pounds butterfish fillets
Olive oil
4 bread slices, crumbled
2 tablespoons slivered almonds
1 tablespoon finely chopped shallots
1 tablespoon chopped parsley
3 cloves garlic, crushed
1/2 teaspoon paprika
1/2 teaspoon finely shredded lemon peel
1 cup tomato purée

1 Rinse fish and pat dry. Lightly oil shallow ovenproof dish. Arrange fish in prepared dish. Brush the top of fish lightly with olive oil.
2 In a small bowl combine crumbled bread, 2 tablespoons of the olive oil, slivered almonds, shallots, parsley, garlic, paprika, and lemon peel. Spoon over fish, pressing mixture firmly into fish.
3 Bake, uncovered, in a 325° oven for 10 minutes. Pour tomato purée over fish. Bake for 10 minutes more or till fish flakes easily when tested with a fork.

–*HORSERADISH*–

Fresh Horseradish

Preparation time:
 5 minutes
Cooking time:
 None
Makes about 1/2 cup

1/3 *cup fresh*
  horseradish roots
3 *tablespoons vinegar*
2 *tablespoons sugar*
2 *teaspoons salt*

1 Wash roots and peel.
Place in a food
processor. Cover and
process till finely
chopped. Add vinegar,
sugar, and salt. Cover
and process till smooth.
Adjust the amount of
vinegar, sugar, and salt,
if desired.
2 Transfer to an
airtight container.
Cover and refrigerate
till serving time.

Serving suggestions
Horseradish is delicious
as an accompaniment
to roast beef and other
grilled meats. Add it to
cream cheese or cottage
cheese to make a tasty
dip or spread.

Pungent horseradish
has many uses in
cooking. Its origins are
obscure, but it is
thought to be one of
the bitter herbs eaten at
the Passover. During
the Middle Ages, both
the leaves and roots
were used in medicine
and as a condiment.
Today it is grown
mainly for the root,
although the young and
tender leaves may be
finely chopped and
added to salads.
  A little horseradish in
spreads and dressings
adds a unique tang.
Horseradish sauce is
a traditional
accompaniment to
roast beef and can also
be served with pork,
chicken, and fish.

23

Horseradish Sour Cream Dressing

Preparation time:
 5 minutes
Cooking time:
 None
Makes about 1 1/2 cups

1 1/4 cups sour cream
3 tablespoons grated
 fresh horseradish or
 2 tablespoons
 prepared horseradish
Salt
Freshly ground pepper

1 In a bowl stir together sour cream and horseradish. Season with salt and pepper.

FRESH HORSERADISH

Freshly grated horseradish gives a piquant tang to seafood sauces, mayonnaise, vinaigrette dressings, dips, spreads, and sour cream for baked potatoes. If you can't find fresh, look for the bottled version at your grocery store.

Rolled Smoked Salmon with Artichoke Hearts and Mushrooms

Preparation time:
10 minutes
Cooking time:
2 minutes
Serves 2

4 *smoked salmon or trout fillets*
4 *ounces soft-style cream cheese*
2 *teaspoons prepared horseradish*
2 *marinated artichoke hearts, halved*
4 *mushroom caps, stems removed*
2 *tablespoons white wine vinegar*
Watercress

1 Place salmon or trout fillets on a plate. In a small bowl stir together cream cheese and horseradish. Using a small metal spatula or table knife dipped in hot water, spread cream cheese mixture over each fillet.
2 Place an artichoke heart half on each fillet. Fold edges over cream cheese filling and partially over artichoke heart. Cover and chill till serving time.

3 Before serving, flute mushroom caps with a knife. In a small saucepan combine mushrooms and vinegar. Add enough water to cover mushrooms. Bring to a boil; reduce heat. Simmer, uncovered, for 2 minutes. Remove mushrooms with a slotted spoon; cool.
4 To serve, place two fillets on an individual serving plate. Arrange two mushrooms near fillets and garnish with watercress. Repeat with remaining fillets, mushrooms, and watercress.

Variations
Canned hearts of palm can replace the artichoke hearts and ricotta cheese can be substituted for the cream cheese.

Serving Suggestions
This recipe makes an ideal main course accompanied by an endive and orange salad and crusty bread.

Rolled Smoked Salmon with Artichoke Hearts and Mushrooms

Which Herb and Spice For What Food?

Anise   *fresh leaves used in salads, steamed vegetables, shellfish; aniseed used in beef, pork, carrots, cakes, cookies, and pastries*

Basil   *used in pesto, tomato dishes, eggs, mushrooms, meat dishes, green salads, pasta, and dips*

Bay leaf   *part of bouquet garni, used in corned beef, stews, soups, pot roast, fish, eggs, dried bean dishes, potatoes, rice, gravies, and marinades*

Caraway   *seeds flavor meat loaves, pot roasts, soups, stews, eggs, stuffings, breads, biscuits, pasta, cabbage, parsnips, turnips, and peas*

Chervil   *part of fines herbes, used with meats, eggs, chicken, fish, salads, soups, and sauces*

Chives   *used in egg dishes, soups, mayonnaise, dips, and sauces*

Coriander   *seeds used in curries, pork, poultry, soups, stews, stuffings, fruit salads, and pickled fruit; fresh leaves used with fish, vegetables, Asian and Southwest dishes*

Dill   *leaves, seeds, and weed goes well with meats, poultry, fish, seafood, soups, salads, white sauces, egg dishes, cheese, and pickles*

Fennel   *fresh leaves and seeds taste good in soups, with fish, meats, cottage cheese, and bread*

Garlic   *used liberally in pasta dishes, meats, poultry, casseroles, soups, stews, sauces, and vegetables*

Ginger   *used in curries, meats, pickles, chutneys, vegetables, cakes, cookies, and bread*

Horseradish	*used to flavor beef, poultry, shellfish, and pork*
Lemongrass	*used extensively in Thai cooking, curries, and salads*
Lovage	*used in soups, stews, salads, and sauces*
Marjoram	*for seasoning Italian dishes, meats, poultry, soups, stews, vegetables, egg dishes, and rice*
Mint	*used with lamb, vegetables, fruit salads, desserts, and iced tea*
Oregano	*used in meat, poultry, fish, and seafood dishes, soups, stews, casseroles, egg dishes, pasta dishes, tomato sauces, and with vegetables*
Parsley	*part of bouquet garni, used in stews, meat dishes, salads, fish, vegetables, and grains*
Sage	*used in stuffings, with poultry, eggs, salads, soups, stews, and breads*
Savory	*used with meats, poultry, fish, soups, stews, egg dishes, sauces, and vegetables*
Sorrel	*used in salads, soups, sauces, and vegetable purées*
Tarragon	*used with chicken, meats, fish, seafood, cream sauces, and vegetables*
Thyme	*used in bouquet garni, casseroles, meat dishes, seafood, eggs, soups, stews, vegetables, salads, breads, and sauces*
Watercress	*used in soups, sauces, salads, and main dish pies*

-MARJORAM-

Marjoram and oregano are closely related. There are slight differences in their appearance and each has its own distinctive flavor. Marjoram is a compact, upright herb with soft grey-green leaves. Oregano, which is really a wild form of marjoram, grows into a bigger plant whose leaves are much firmer than marjoram leaves.

Patted Potato Parcels

Preparation time:
15 minutes
Cooking time:
30 minutes
Serves 6

4 *medium potatoes*
2 *tablespoons milk*
1 *tablespoon self-rising flour*
3 *strips bacon*
1 *small onion, finely chopped*
1 *medium apple, peeled and finely shredded*
1 *tablespoon chopped fresh marjoram*
Salt
Freshly ground pepper
1 *tablespoon cooking oil*

1 Peel and quarter potatoes. Cook in boiling water for 20 minutes or till tender. Drain. Mash potatoes with milk till smooth. Add flour and mash till well combined. Divide mixture into 6 portions.
2 In a skillet cook finely chopped bacon till crisp. Drain on paper towel, reserving drippings. Cook onion in bacon drippings till tender and brown. Add apple and marjoram and cook for 1 minute. Return bacon to skillet. Season with salt and pepper.
3 With your hands, flatten each portion of potatoes into a flat circle. Add 1 tablespoon bacon mixture to center of each circle. Bring edges up around bacon mixture; fold and press edges to seal. Gently press each portion of potato again into a flattened circle.
4 In same skillet heat oil over medium heat. Add potato patties and cook till light brown on both sides.

Patted Potato Parcels

Cook's Tip
Chill uncooked patties for 1 hour to allow them to firm so they are easier to handle.

Serving Suggestions
Serve patties with meat, fish, or poultry or serve as a light lunch with a fresh garden salad.

Variations
Use other flavoring ingredients such as grated Parmesan cheese and caraway seed.

–*Mint*–

–*Mint*–

MARJORAM VS. OREGANO

The fragrance of marjoram is soft and gentle which makes it an excellent herb to combine with other herbs. Oregano has a pungent dominant flavor and is best used alone or with other strong herbs such as basil.

USES

Marjoram is an ingredient in traditional mixed herbs along with thyme and sage. It is a useful herb for many mixtures where subtle flavor is desired. It also has great value on its own. Marjoram goes well with poultry, fish, eggs, vegetables, and sauces. Use fresh or dried leaves in dumplings and savory scones. The fresh leaves are delicious torn into green salads. When carefully stripped from their stalks, they don't need chopping.

These days, there is a bewildering selection of mints on the market, all with unique scents and flavors.

Spearmint is the variety which gives mint sauces a wonderful flavor. It is also popular for mint jellies and mint juleps. Chopped spearmint enlivens buttered new potatoes, green peas, and tomatoes. Sprinkle it on hot or chilled pea or avocado soup. Mint is nice with egg dishes, lamb, fruit salads, and puddings.

Herbed Cheese Log

Preparation time:
  12 minutes
Cooking time:
  None
Chilling time:
  30 minutes
Serves 4

Herbed Cheese Log

8 *ounces cream cheese,*
6 *ounces ricotta cheese*
2 *cups shredded*
  Monterey Jack cheese
2 *tablespoons chopped*
  pitted ripe olives
2 *tablespoon chopped*
  pitted green olives
2 *shallots, chopped*
1 *teaspoon Tabasco*
  sauce
Pinch ground red pepper
3 *tablespoons finely*
  chopped fresh mint
1 *tablespoon poppy seed*
1 *tablespoon sesame*
  seed

1 In a bowl beat softened cream cheese and ricotta cheese with an electric mixer till smooth. Add Monterey Jack cheese, olives, shallots, Tabasco, and pepper and beat till well combined.

2 On a large piece of waxed paper or foil combine mint, poppy seed, and sesame seed. Shape mixture into a log and roll in mint mixture till well coated.

3 Roll log tightly in plastic wrap. Seal and chill at least 30 minutes. Cut into slices to serve.

Serving Suggestions
Serve this savory cheese log with crackers or crusty bread slices. It's great with pre-dinner drinks or as a satisfying snack.

31

Stuffed Lamb and Cabbage Rolls

Preparation time:
  15 minutes
Cooking time:
  1 hour
Serves 6

12 *medium to large
  cabbage leaves*
1 *pound lean ground
  lamb or beef*
*1/2 cup uncooked long
  grain rice*
3 *cloves garlic, crushed*
*3/4 teaspoon ground
  cinnamon*
Pinch allspice
Salt
Freshly ground pepper
Juice of 1 lemon
1 *clove garlic, crushed*
2 *tablespoons chopped
  fresh mint*
Plain yogurt
*Red bell pepper slivers
  or shredded red
  cabbage*

1 Remove center vein
from cabbages, leaving
leaf in one piece.
Immerse leaves in
boiling water for
1 minute. Drain and
rinse with cold water.
2 In a bowl stir
together meat, rice,
garlic, cinnamon, and
allspice. Season with salt
and pepper. Place about
1/4 cup of meat mixture
on each cabbage leaf;
fold in sides. Starting at
an unfolded edge,
carefully roll up each

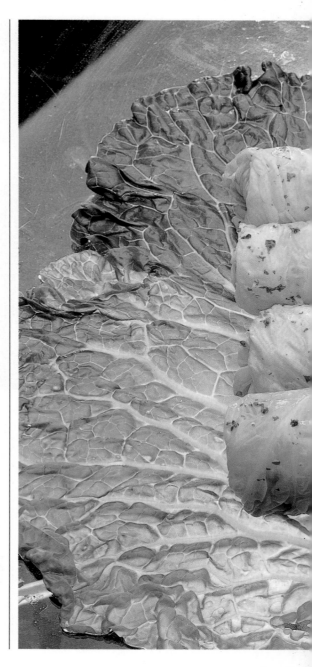

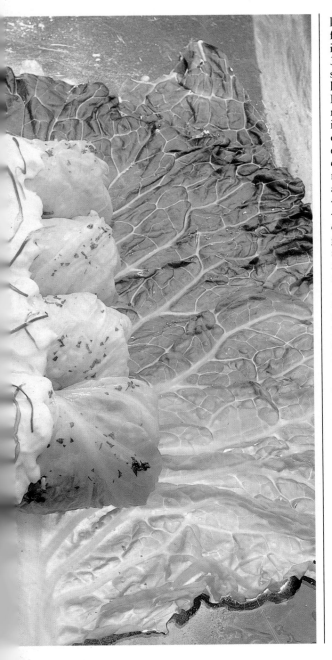

leaf, making sure the folded sides are included in roll.

3 Place cabbage rolls, seam side down, in a large saucepan or Dutch oven. To prevent rolls from floating, invert a small plate over rolls and add enough water to cover. Bring to a boil; reduce heat. Cover and simmer for 45 minutes.

4 In a small bowl combine lemon juice, garlic, and mint; add to saucepan with cabbage rolls. Continue cooking for 15 minutes more.

5 To serve, remove rolls and arrange on a serving plate. Spoon yogurt over the top and garnish with red bell pepper or cabbage.

Cook's Tip
This is a great cook-ahead meal for busy work days. Cover the finished dish and store in the refrigerator for up to two days or freeze for several days.

Stuffed Lamb and Cabbage Rolls

Mint and Ginger Green Beans

Preparation time:
  5 minutes
Cooking time:
  15 minutes
Serves 4

*¹/₂-inch piece gingerroot,
  finely shredded*
*1 pound fresh green
  beans, trimmed*
*2 tablespoons finely
  chopped fresh mint*
1 teaspoon olive oil
Fresh mint sprigs

1 In a saucepan add
enough water to just
cover bottom. Bring to
a boil; reduce heat. Add
gingerroot and simmer
for 2 minutes.
2 Add beans and mint.
Return to a boil; reduce
heat. Cover; simmer for
15 minutes or till crisp-
tender. Cover; chill till
serving (do not drain).
3 To serve, toss chilled
bean mixture with olive
oil. Garnish with fresh
mint.

Mint Sambal

Preparation time:
  5 minutes

1 cup fresh mint leaves
1 medium onion, peeled
¹/₂ cup plain yogurt
*1 fresh green chili
  (optional)*

Mint and Ginger Green Beans

1 In a blender combine mint and onion. Blend till finely chopped. Add yogurt. Blend till creamy. If desired, add chili and blend till well combined.
2 Serve with curries or barbecued chicken.

Serving Suggestion
This mixture can be used as a marinade for chicken by adding chopped gingerroot and ground turmeric.

Mint Vinegar

Preparation time:
  10 minutes
Standing time:
  2 weeks

¹/₂ cup fresh mint leaves
2 tablespoons chopped fresh chives
8 whole black peppercorns
2 thin slices fresh chili
2 cups white wine vinegar

1 In a clean glass jar combine mint, chives, peppercorns, and chili. Add vinegar and seal.
2 Keep at room temperature in a cool, dark place 2 weeks. Before using, strain. Add fresh mint sprigs, a few chives, and a few peppercorns.

–OREGANO–

Oregano is really a wild form of marjoram and plays a different role from marjoram because of its dominant pungent taste. It is used extensively in ethnic regional dishes, especially in Italy where it appears in pasta dishes, rice dishes, and pizzas. It combines well with tomatoes, zucchini, bell peppers, and eggplant. Try sprinkling some dried oregano on lamb or pork before roasting.

Baked Tortellini

Preparation time:
  15 minutes
Cooking time:
  30 minutes
Serves 4

1 large eggplant
Salt
8 or 9 ounces
  refrigerated cheese- or
  chicken-filled tortellini
2 medium potatoes,
  peeled and cut into
  ³/₄-inch thick slices
¹/₂ cup olive oil

1 medium onion, thinly
  sliced
14¹/₂-ounce can whole
  tomatoes
¹/₂ teaspoon chopped
  fresh oregano
Pinch ground red
  pepper
Salt
Freshly ground pepper

Baked Tortellini

In a large skillet heat
half of the olive oil.
Cook potatoes in hot
skillet till brown on
both sides. Place in dish
with tortellini, tossing
gently to mix.
4 In same saucepan
heat remaining oil.
Cook onion in skillet
till tender. Add
eggplant and cook
5 minutes more or till
eggplant is brown,
adding more oil if
necessary during
cooking.
5 Partially drain
tomatoes and add them
to skillet with eggplant
mixture, breaking
tomatoes up with a
wooden spoon. Add
oregano and ground
red pepper. Season with
salt and pepper. Cook
for 5 to 8 minutes more
or till most of liquid is
evaporated.
6 Add eggplant-tomato
mixture to tortellini
mixture in dish. Add 1/3
cup of the Romano
cheese and stir gently
till well combined.
Sprinkle with
remaining cheese and
additional oregano.
7 Bake, uncovered,
in a 375° oven for
10 minutes or till
cheese melts and pasta
is heated through.

*1 cup shredded
  Romano cheese
Chopped fresh oregano*

1 Chop eggplant into
3/4-inch pieces. Place
in a colander and
sprinkle with salt. Place
over the sink and let
drain while preparing

the other ingredients.
2 Cook tortellini
according to package
directions; drain. Place
in a lightly oiled
ovenproof dish.
3 In a small saucepan
boil potato slices in
water about 5 minutes
or till just tender; drain.

–PARSLEY–

Parsley leaves, whether fresh or dried, go into sauces, scrambled eggs, omelettes, mashed potatoes, cream sauces, salads, soups, pasta, vegetables, poultry, and fish. Curly leaf parsley can be washed, thoroughly dried, and quickly fried in butter till crisp for a tasty accompaniment to grilled fish. Flat leaf parsley goes particularly well with Italian dishes.

Smoked Fish Flan

Preparation time:
  20 minutes
Cooking time:
  30 minutes
Serves 4

1 small onion, sliced
1/4 cup water

38

Smoked Fish Flan

2 Brush each sheet of phyllo dough with the 3 tablespoons melted butter. Fold each sheet in half. On a flat surface layer phyllo dough, one folded piece on top of the other, to get 8 layers.
3 Using an 8-inch flan ring as a guide, cut out a circle from phyllo dough that is 2 inches larger than the flan ring. Carefully lift and place phyllo dough into flan pan, allowing pastry to stand up around the edge. Trim pastry, if necessary.
4 In a saucepan melt the 2 tablespoons butter. Stir in flour. Add milk. Cook and stir till thickened. Cook and stir 1 minute more.
5 In a small bowl stir together egg, anchovy paste, and 1 tablespoon parsley. Add a small amount of sauce to egg mixture. Return all egg mixture to saucepan. Cook and stir over low heat till heated through. Remove from heat. Season to taste with salt and pepper. Stir in lemon juice.
6 Spread fish and onion over phyllo dough in the bottom of the flan pan. Pour sauce over. Bake, uncovered, in 350° oven for 30 minutes or until knife comes out clean.

1/4 cup dry sherry
8 ounces smoked fish fillets, flaked
4 sheets phyllo dough
3 tablespoons butter, melted
2 tablespoons butter
2 tablespoons all-purpose flour
1 cup milk
1 egg, beaten
1/2 teaspoon anchovy paste

1 tablespoon chopped fresh parsley
Salt
Freshly ground pepper
1 teaspoon lemon juice
Chopped fresh parsley

1 In a saucepan combine onion, water, and sherry. Bring to boil; reduce heat. Simmer, uncovered, for 10 minutes. Add fish.

Herbed Vegetable Ring

Preparation time:
  15 minutes
Cooking time:
  30 to 35 minutes
Serves 4 to 6

3 carrots, shredded
1 large leek, cleaned
  and sliced
1 cup shredded cheddar
  or Gruyère cheese
1/2 cup all-purpose
  flour
1/3 cup cooking oil
3 tablespoons chopped
  fresh parsley
2 tablespoons chopped
  fresh chives
1 tablespoon chopped
  fresh dill or
  1 teaspoon dried
  dillweed
1/4 teaspoon baking
  powder
Salt
Freshly ground pepper
4 eggs, separated

1 In a bowl combine
carrots, leek, shredded
cheese, flour, cooking
oil, parsley, chives, dill,
and baking powder.
Season with salt and
pepper. Stir in egg yolks.
Beat egg whites till stiff
peaks form; fold into
egg yolk mixture.
2 Spoon into a greased
10-inch tube pan;
smooth surface. Bake
in a 350° oven for
30 to 35 minutes or
till brown.
3 To serve, unmold
onto a serving plate.
Serve with a fresh
green salad.

Variations
Any number of
vegetable and herb
combinations can be
used in the recipe
above, depending on
vegetable and herb
availability and the
imagination of the
cook.

Watchpoint
When folding beaten
egg whites into a
mixture, stir in
1 tablespoon of the
beaten egg white, then
fold remaining whites
into mixture. This will
lighten the mixture
before folding in all the
egg whites.

Herbed Vegetable Ring

-ROSEMARY-

Herbed Lamb Salad

Preparation time:
  10 minutes
Cooking time:
  25 to 30 minutes
Serves 6

Cooking oil
1¹/2 pounds lean
  boneless lamb loin

Vinaigrette
1 tablespoon Dijon
  mustard
1 tablespoon white
  wine vinegar
¹/4 cup olive oil
Salt
Freshly ground pepper
¹/2 head red cabbage,
  shredded
1 tablespoon caraway
  seed
1 tablespoon chopped
  fresh rosemary
2 tablespoons pine
  nuts, lightly toasted

This herb is one of the
most pungent, with a
warm resinous scent.
Rosemary gives a
savory tang to beef,
lamb, veal, poultry,
pork, rabbit, goose, and
duck. It is used in pâtés
and pasta sauces with
great success. Try
sprinkling a few
chopped fresh leaves on
fresh tomatoes or
cooked vegetables such
as grilled eggplant.

1 In a skillet heat oil
over medium-high heat.
Brown lamb in hot
skillet on all sides. Place
in a shallow roasting
pan. Roast in a
350° oven for 25 to
30 minutes or till meat
thermometer registers
140° to 145° for
medium rare. Remove
and let stand.
2 For vinaigrette, in a

Herbed Lamb Salad

bowl whisk together
mustard and vinegar.
Slowly add oil,
whisking till well
combined. Season with
salt and pepper.
3 To assemble, in a
bowl toss together
cabbage and warmed
vinaigrette. Stir in
caraway seed and
rosemary. Arrange
on a serving plate
and top with slices of
lamb. Sprinkle with
pine nuts.

Cook's Tip
For best results, place
meat on a roasting
rack in a roasting pan
and turn the meat over
halfway through
roasting for even
heating. Once the
meat is cooked, wrap
it in foil and let stand
15 minutes before
cutting.

Savory Scone Roll

Preparation time:
20 minutes
Cooking time:
20 minutes
Serves 6

Dough
3 cups all-purpose flour
1 1/2 teaspoons baking
  powder
Pinch ground red
  pepper
1/4 cup butter or
  margarine
1 cup milk

Filling
2 slices bacon, cooked
  crisp and crumbled
1 cup shredded cheddar
  cheese
1 tablespoon chopped
  fresh rosemary
1 tablespoon coarse
  grain mustard
1/2 teaspoon paprika
1 egg, beaten

1 For dough, in a large
bowl combine flour,
baking powder, and red
pepper. Cut in butter or
margarine with a pastry
blender till mixture
resembles coarse
crumbs. Make a well in
the center and add
milk. Stir till a soft
dough forms.
2 On a lightly floured
surface knead dough till
smooth. Roll dough
into a 12 x 10-inch
rectangle. Combine
bacon, cheese,

rosemary, mustard, and paprika. Sprinkle over dough. Starting at a long end, roll up dough jelly-roll style. Seal ends and seams.

3 Place dough, seam side down, on a greased baking sheet. Brush with beaten egg.

4 Bake in a 400° oven for 20 minutes or till golden brown. Slice and serve warm.

Variations
One teaspoon dried rosemary can replace the fresh in these tender scones. Use pepperoni instead of bacon, tomato paste instead of mustard, chopped olives, and dried basil and you've turned this into a pizza-flavored filling for your scone.

Cook's Tip
Always preheat your oven for 10 minutes at the specified temperature in the recipes. This is particularly important when baking breads and pastries because the dough needs to crisp or brown.

FRESH OR DRY
You can purchase fresh or dried rosemary all year round at most large supermarkets. To dry fresh rosemary, harvest the rosemary before the plant begins to flower because the flavor will be best. Tie the stalks together and hang them in a shady, airy place. When dry, strip leaves from stems and crumble into small pieces. Store in an airtight container for several months.

STORING
Besides drying, rosemary can also be stored in the freezer for a few months. Or, use rosemary to make fresh herb butter and store in your refrigerator till needed. Rosemary should always be finely chopped or ground with a mortar and pestle to make the stiff leaves

Savory Scone Roll

–*SAGE*–

Sage is a traditional ingredient in a mixed herb blend with thyme and marjoram. Use sage on its own or combine it with other herbs. Use it to season pork, goose, duck, veal, and fish. Cook sage with beans, peas, onions, eggplant, tomatoes, vegetable soups, cheese and egg dishes, dumplings, scones, and rich cream sauces.

SAGE TIPS
Sage and rosemary aid each other when they are planted in the same garden. Plant sage next to cabbage since sage improves the flavor of cabbage and helps repel harmful cabbage butterflies.

Sage and Mushrooms with Linguine

Sage and Mushrooms with Linguine

Preparation time:
  5 minutes
Cooking time:
  15 minutes
Serves 4

12 ounces linguine
3 tablespoons butter
1 small onion, finely
  chopped
12 ounces mushrooms,
  sliced
1 tablespoon chopped
  fresh sage
1 tablespoon chopped
  fresh parsley
Salt
Freshly ground pepper
1/4 cup grated
  Parmesan cheese

1 Cook linguine according to package directions; drain.
2 In a saucepan melt butter. Add onion and cook till tender. Stir in mushrooms, sage, and parsley. Cover and cook over low heat for 10 minutes. Season with salt and pepper.
3 Pour mushroom mixture over linguine, tossing to coat. Sprinkle with Parmesan cheese.

Watchpoint
One teaspoon dried sage can be used to replace the fresh.

Saltimbocca

Preparation time:
  10 minutes
Cooking time:
  15 minutes
Serves 6

12 *veal scallops*
12 *fresh sage leaves*
12 *slices ham*
12 *slices mozzarella*
  cheese
All-purpose flour
1/3 *cup butter*
1 *cup dry white wine*
Salt
Freshly ground pepper

1 Place veal between
2 sheets of plastic wrap
and pound with the flat
side of a meat mallet till
as thin as possible.
Place 1 sage leaf, 1 slice
ham, and 1 slice cheese
on each piece of veal.
Fold in half and secure
with toothpicks. Coat
with flour.
2 In a large skillet heat
butter over medium-
high heat. Add veal;
cook for 5 minutes on
each side. Remove from
skillet; keep warm.
3 Add wine to skillet.
Cook and stir over
medium-high heat,
scraping up brown bits.
Season with salt and
pepper. Pour over veal.

Variations
Do not substitute dried
sage for fresh in this
flavorful veal dish.

–SORREL–

French sorrel grows in
thick clumps like
spinach. The broad
long leaves are light
green and have a
pleasant acid taste.

A well-known use for
sorrel is in soup – a
favorite in French
cuisine. Delicious sorrel
sauce is excellent with
cold poultry, terrines,
hot boiled potatoes,
omelettes, and lamb
chops. Toss the young
tender leaves into a
salad with mild-tasting
greens.

Salmon with Sorrel Cream Sauce

Preparation time:
  8 minutes
Cooking time:
  15 minutes
Serves 4

4 *salmon steaks*
Freshly ground pepper
1/4 *cup unsalted butter*
  or margarine

Sorrel Cream Sauce
1/4 *cup unsalted butter*
  or margarine

Salmon with Sorrel Cream Sauce

Remove from heat and stir in lemon juice. Season with salt and pepper.

3 Place salmon on individual serving plates. Spoon warm sauce over salmon. Garnish with fresh sorrel.

Cook's Tip
Instead of frying, you can steam the salmon on a bed of sorrel over simmering water.

Note
If salmon is not available, use halibut or swordfish steaks.

Variation
Thinly slice the cooked fish and stir into sauce. Serve hot over a bed of hot cooked pasta.

2 shallots, chopped
1 cup whipping cream
8 sorrel leaves, stemmed and sliced into strips
Juice of 1/2 lemon
Salt
Freshly ground pepper
Sorrel leaves

1 Rinse fish and pat dry with paper towels. Season with pepper. In a large skillet heat 1/4 cup butter or margarine over medium-high heat. Cook salmon in hot skillet for 3 to 4 minutes per side or till the fish flakes easily when tested with a fork.

2 For sauce, in a saucepan melt 1/4 cup butter or margarine. Cook shallots in butter till tender. Add cream. Bring to a boil; reduce heat. Simmer for 1 minute. Add sorrel and simmer for 2 minutes more.

–*Tarragon*–

French tarragon is native to the Mediterranean and has become very popular in continental cooking. The name tarragon is adapted from the French "estragon", which in turn is derived from the Latin "dracunculus", meaning little dragon. The herb was known as a cure for venomous bites and stings along with having the reputation of being "a friend to the head, heart, and liver."

Tarragon has a unique anise aroma with long narrow leaves. Another form of tarragon called winter tarragon is also available. It is sturdier than the French version with a strong and spicy flavor and aroma. Winter tarragon makes a good substitute for the more tender French tarragon.

Pears in Tarragon Sauce

Preparation time:
  5 minutes
Cooking time:
  8 to 10 minutes
Serves 6

3 ripe pears
Lettuce leaves
Paprika

Pears in Tarragon Dressing

sauce over pears, coating pears completely. Sprinkle with paprika.

Variations
If desired, poach pears gently in a sugar and water syrup until just tender.
Apples can be substituted for the pears and prepared as directed in the recipe.

HINT

The core of the pear can be removed quickly and easily with a melon baller.

Cook's Tip
Brush peeled pears with lemon juice or sprinkle with fruit fresh to prevent them from turning brown.

Sauce
1 egg
2 tablespoons sugar
3 tablespoons tarragon
  vinegar
Salt
Freshly ground pepper
2 cups plain yogurt

1 For sauce, in the top of a double boiler combine egg and sugar. Whisk in vinegar. Cook and stir till mixture starts to thicken. Remove from heat and whisk till mixture is the consistency of thick cream. Season with salt and pepper; cool. Stir in yogurt.
2 To serve, peel, core, and halve pears lengthwise. Arrange lettuce leaves on 6 individual salad plates. Place pears, cut side down, on top of lettuce leaves. Spoon

-*THYME*-

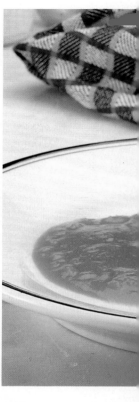

The scent of thyme evokes thoughts of good things cooking in the oven or hearty soups simmering on the stove. The special fragrance of thyme goes into many dishes and is an essential ingredient in herb blends with sage and marjoram or in bouquet garni with parsley and bay leaf.

The pungent flavor of thyme is indispensable in soups, stews, casseroles, meat loaves, stuffings, sauces, marinades, and pâtés. It gives a delicious savory flavor to bread and cooked vegetables. Lemon thyme, with a milder aroma, is excellent with fish, chicken, steamed carrots, and cream sauces.

Timbales Indienne with Tangy Tomato Sauce

Preparation time:
  12 to 15 minutes
Cooking time:
  30 minutes
Serves 4

1 pound boneless
  skinless chicken breasts
6 ounces ham
1 cup cooked long
  grain rice

Timbales Indienne with Tangy Tomato Sauce

Bake in a 350° oven for 30 minutes or till done.
3 Meanwhile, for sauce, in a small saucepan combine tomato purée, onion, wine or broth, and chopped thyme. Bring to a boil; reduce heat. Simmer for 10 minutes, stirring occasionally. Keep warm.
4 To serve, spoon sauce onto individual serving plates. Unmold timbales onto plates. Garnish with escarole.

Variations
You can substitute fish, shrimp, lamb, or pork for the chicken in these tasty timbales. Go ahead and use one large mold instead of 4 molds or custard cups, but add several minutes to baking time.

Serving Suggestions
For a great summer lunch or picnic serve slices of chilled timbale with tomato sauce and include a crisp green salad.

Cook's Tip
You can prepare timbales the day before serving. Cover and store them assembled, but uncooked, in the refrigerator until ready to bake.

1 *small onion, chopped*
1 *small green bell pepper, finely chopped*
1 *egg, beaten*
1 *clove garlic, crushed*
1 *teaspoon curry powder*
Salt
Freshly ground pepper

Sauce
8-ounce can tomato purée
1 *small onion, finely chopped*
2 *tablespoons dry white wine or chicken broth*

1 *tablespoon finely chopped fresh thyme*
Escarole

1 In a food processor combine chicken and ham. Cover and process till finely chopped. Transfer to a bowl and stir in rice, onion, bell pepper, egg, garlic, and curry powder. Season with salt and pepper.
2 Spoon mixture into 4 timbale molds or custard cups. Place on a baking sheet.

–WATERCRESS–

A perennial plant with dark green, fleshy leaves with a live, peppery taste. If you don't grown your own, watercress is usually sold in small bunches all year round in your grocer's produce section. Choose healthy looking stems with bright green leaves.

STORING
Store watercress in damp paper towels in a plastic bag in the refrigerator for up to 2 days.

Herbed Chicken Pie

Preparation time:
  15 minutes
Cooking time:
  30 to 35 minutes
Serves 4

Filling
1/4 cup butter or margarine
3 tablespoons all-purpose flour
2 tablespoons finely chopped fresh thyme
1 clove garlic, finely chopped
2 tablespoons chopped fresh watercress
Salt
Freshly ground pepper
1 cup milk
2 cups chopped cooked chicken
1 cup assorted vegetable strips such as carrot, celery, or zucchini, blanched
1/2 cup dry white wine
1/2 cup whipping cream
17 1/4-ounce package (2 sheets) frozen puff pastry, thawed
1 beaten egg
Watercress sprigs

1 For filling, in a saucepan melt butter or margarine over medium heat. Stir in flour, thyme,

Herbed Chicken Pie

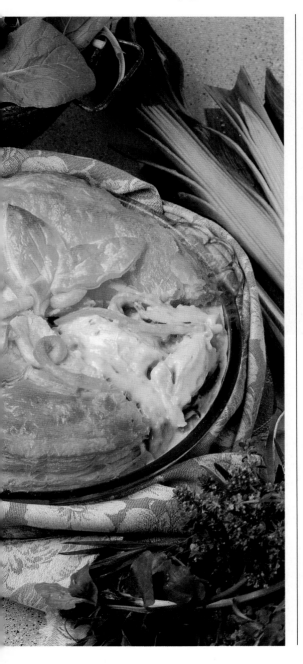

garlic, and watercress. Season with salt and pepper. Add milk. Cook and stir till thickened and bubbly. Cook and stir 1 minute more. Remove from heat and add chicken, vegetables, wine, and cream.

2 Line a 9-inch pie plate with one sheet of the pastry. Trim edges. Pour in chicken filling. Moisten edge of pastry with water. Top with remaining sheet of pastry. Trim edges with a sharp knife. Brush with beaten egg and pierce with a fork to allow steam to escape.

3 Bake in a 400° oven for 30 to 35 minutes or till golden brown. Serve warm and garnish with watercress.

Variations
Replace the chicken with salmon or tuna, if preferred.

Cook's Tip
This is another recipe to keep in mind for busy days. Assemble the pie; cover and refrigerate it without cooking for up to 2 days.

USES
Watercress leaves are delicious in sandwiches instead of lettuce. Try them in salads, soups, and main dish pies.

Watercress Soup

Watercress Soup

Preparation time:
8 minutes
Cooking time:
30 minutes
Serves 4

1 bunch watercress
2 tablespoons butter or
  margarine
2 onions, chopped
1 large potato, peeled
  and diced
Salt
Freshly ground pepper
2½ cups chicken broth
2 tablespoons all-
  purpose flour
⅔ cup light cream

1 Reserve a few stalks of watercress for garnish. Chop remaining watercress. In a heavy saucepan melt 2 tablespoons butter or margarine. Stir in onions, potato, and watercress. Season with salt and pepper. Cover and simmer for 10 minutes.

2 Add chicken broth to saucepan. Bring to a boil; reduce heat. Simmer for 15 minutes. Transfer to a food processor or blender container. Cover and process or blend till smooth. Strain into a bowl.

3 Clean saucepan.

Melt 2 tablespoons butter or margarine in saucepan. Stir in flour. Return soup to saucepan. Stir in cream. Cook and stir till thickened and bubbly. Cook and stir 1 minute more. Serve hot or cold garnished with reserved watercress.

Variations
If watercress is not available, use fresh parsley or sorrel instead. If you're counting calories, use evaporated skim milk instead of light cream.

Supreme Asparagus Salad

cool; drain. Cover and
chill till serving time.
2 For dressing, stir
together watercress,
sour cream, lemon
juice, and chives.
Season with white
pepper.
3 To serve, place
asparagus on individual
serving plates. Spoon
dressing over
asparagus. Garnish
with watercress.

Watchpoint
For the freshest-tasting
results, do not
overcook asparagus.
Cook it only till it is
crisp-tender.

Variations
Fresh broccoli spears
make a good substitute
for the asparagus
spears.

Supreme Asparagus Salad

Preparation time:
  5 minutes
Cooking time:
  15 minutes
Serves 4

1¹/2 *pounds fresh
  asparagus, trimmed*

Dressing
1 *bunch watercress,
  finely chopped*
¹/4 *cup sour cream*
2 *tablespoons lemon
  juice*
2 *tablespoons chopped
  fresh chives*
Ground white pepper

1 Cook asparagus in
boiling water for
3–4 minutes or till just
crisp-tender. Drain and
plunge in ice water to

-TIPS & HINTS-

FRESHEN UP YOUR CLOTHES

To give clothes a fresh outdoor smell, use herbal packets when you do the laundry. Tie up six tablespoons of your favorite dried herbs in the foot cut from an old pair of pantyhose. Add this to your washing machine during the rinse cycle, then put it in the dryer along with your wet clothes. The herbs will dry with the clothes to give them a fresh aroma. If desired, the herb packet can be reused.

MINTY BREEZES

On a hot day, place a bowl of ice and crushed mint in front of a fan for a cool, minty breeze.

AVOID CHEMICALS

When selecting herbs to use in cooking or eating, never use any that have been sprayed with pesticides or insecticides. Always rinse off the herbs and pat dry with paper towels before using.

HERB CROUTONS

Remove the crusts from slices of bread and cut into cubes. Cook the bread cubes in a skillet with butter or margarine, minced garlic, and finely chopped fresh herbs. Cook and stir till bread is crisp. Drain on paper towels. Sprinkle in salads or on soups.

HERBED NOODLES

For a quick and easy herb sauce, buy a purchased refrigerated cream sauce from your supermarket and stir in a few tablespoons of chopped fresh herbs while you reheat it. Toss it with hot cooked noodles or pasta.

HERB BUTTER

In a food processor or blender container combine butter or margarine and chopped fresh herbs. Cover and process or blend till smooth. Transfer to a storage container or shape into a log and chill till needed.

HOW TO DRY HERBS

Here are two easy ways to dry fresh herbs. In general, the faster the herbs dry, the more flavorful the resulting dried herbs will be.

Conventional oven:
Place clean dry herb sprigs on a foil-lined baking sheet. Bake at the lowest setting until herbs are dry and brittle. This should take about 12 hours. Strip leaves from stems, place in a small airtight storage containers.

Air drying:
Tie small bunches of herbs with string and hang them upside down by the stems in a dry warm spot out of direct sunlight. Be sure air circulates freely around the bunches. Let dry till leaves are brittle. This usually takes a few days to a week, depending on the thickness of the leaves. Pick off the dried leaves and store in tightly covered containers in a cool, dry place about 2 weeks or till dry and brittle.

HOW TO STORE HERBS

Sprigs of fresh herbs or freshly chopped herbs wrapped in foil or plastic wrap can be stored in the refrigerator for nearly a week. To keep for longer periods, finely chop clean herbs, place in ice cube trays and fill trays with water. Freeze till frozen solid. When needed, remove herb ice cubes and drop into hot cooking liquid — they will melt and flavor the dish. Since freezing may make the herbs stronger tasting and a bit bitter, use a little less of the frozen herbs than you would fresh. You can also wrap bunches of fresh herbs in foil or plastic wrap and freeze them for several weeks. You should expect some discoloration of frozen herbs.

Another method of storing herbs is to stir finely chopped fresh herbs into softened butter or margarine. Spread this mixture in a thin layer on a plate and refrigerate till firm. Then cut into squares, place in a freezer bag, and freeze till needed.

For dried herbs, mark each container with the date you purchased it. After 1 year, discard any remaining herbs and replace with a new container. Keep dried herbs in tightly covered containers in a cool, dry place. Heat, moisture, and light rob herbs of flavor.

HERBS AND THE GRILL

There are many ways to use herbs when you grill. Here are a few suggestions.

Sprinkle fresh herbs directly on the hot coals before adding the food. Then cover the food while it grills to allow the herb smoke to flavor the meat as it cooks. Try stalks of savory, rosemary, sage, or fennel.

When grilling kabobs, skewer fresh herbs between the pieces of meat and vegetables. Choose oregano with fish or beef, dill with fish or chicken, or basil with beef or pork.

Wrap a fresh ear of corn and a sprig of fresh marjoram in foil and roast together on the grill.

Create an herb brush by tying together a few sprigs of fresh herbs. Use it to brush marinade or melted butter over foods as they grill.

Wrap fish in foil with fresh lemon slices and few sprigs of fresh dill. Grill till fish flakes easily with a fork.

HERBS AND SALADS

Fresh herbs bring new life to salads. Tear sorrel, watercress, and basil leaves into pieces and mix them with torn lettuce. For strong herbs like savory, dill, and thyme, chop them before adding to salads.

Fennel seeds tossed in salads add pockets of spice.

Fruit salad is cool and refreshing when served on a bed of fresh leafy mint.

HOW TO SUBSTITUTE

To substitute fresh herbs for dried herbs in recipes, use three times the amount of fresh herb as dried herb. For example, use 1 tablespoon of a chopped fresh herb or 1 teaspoon of the dried herb, crushed.

HOW TO RELEASE FLAVORS

To release the flavor of fresh herbs, chop or snip them beforehand. When using a dried herb, measure it first, then crush it in the palm of your hand to release the aromatic oils and flavor. Or, place herbs in the bottom of mortar or small bowl. Use a pestle or the back of a small spoon to crush the leaves. If you are using your own dried herbs, crush them slightly before measuring.

NUTRITIOUS HERBS

Fresh and dried herbs contain no calories, fat, or sodium. That makes them a healthy choice to use in cooking.

HERB VINEGARS

Here's how to make your own herb vinegar to use in salad dressing or marinades. Place 2 cups packed fresh tarragon, thyme, dill, or basil into a hot, clean 1-quart jar. In a stainless steel or enamel saucepan heat 2 cups wine vinegar till hot but not boiling. Pour hot vinegar into jar over herbs. Cover loosely with the lid or waxed paper till vinegar cools. Then cover tightly with the lid. Let vinegar stand in a cool, dark place for 1 week. Remove herb from jar and transfer vinegar to a clean dry 2-cup jar. Add a sprig of the fresh herb to the vinegar, if desired. Cover and store in a cool, dark place for up to 3 months.

HOW TO ADD HERBS TO BEVERAGES

Add zest to everyday beverages by using herbs.

Garnish lemonade with lemon thyme or mint, tomato juice with oregano or basil, and mineral water and iced tea with mint.

Make herbal teas by steeping two to three tablespoons dried leafy herbs such as mint, marjoram, or borage for each cup tea. Serve the herb teas hot or cold.

For festive and flavorful ice cubes, freeze a small sprig of fresh herb in each ice cube tray.

INDEX

Numbers in italics represent recipe pictured.